Power Play

Poems by Mair De-Gare Pitt

Images by Jill Powell

with an Introduction by
Jonathan Edwards

The most precious thing...in the sharp ebb and flow of the revolutionary waves is the proletariat's spiritual growth.
—Rosa Luxemburg

First published 2018 by **Culture Matters.**
Culture Matters Co-Operative Ltd. promotes a socialist
and progressive approach to art, culture and politics. We run
a website which publishes creative and critical material on
politics and culture; manage Bread and Roses arts awards;
deliver cultural education workshops to trade unionists; publish
books; and contribute to the development of culture policy in
the labour movement.
See www.culturematters.org.uk

Edited by Mike Quille
Layout and typesetting by Alan Morrison
ISBN 978-1-912710-05-8

Acknowledgements
Some of these poems have appeared in *Red Poets, Quintet
and other poets* (Cinnamon Press), *Envoi, Orbis, Planet,
Paradox* (Paragram), *Militant Thistles, The Recusant,*
and *On Fighting On* (Culture Matters, 2017).

Introduction to the poems

By Jonathan Edwards

What is politics? When I was a younger person, growing up in the South Wales Valleys in the late 1980s, a far-off and mythical land where cornflakes were splashed not with milk but rather with stories of the Miners' Strike, where usually sober, chapel-going ladies saw Margaret Thatcher on the television and hissed at her like cats, where the songs of the Manic Street Preachers boomed through bedroom windows into terraced streets, and nobody knew what they were saying, and liked it—when I was a younger person, I thought I knew exactly what politics was. It was people shouting at each other.

At the age of fourteen or so, my political career reached its peak, when I met Lord David Sutch, lead singer of the Monster Raving Loony Party, in a local pub. Here, I felt, was the future. My house, conveniently located next to a polling station, offered the perfect site for campaigning on his behalf. My mother would not allow his leaflets in the living room window, and I was banned from actively picketing in the street so, come election day, I plastered my bedroom window with his posters, and sat there on the windowsill, shouting down at people on their way to vote, 'Look up here!' Some of them did. Lord David Sutch did not retain his deposit.

Now I am older and less wise, the importance of politics is much clearer, and it's taken me a good old while to grasp what was clear to others from the start. Politics isn't people shouting at each other. It *is* people. The drowning of Capel Celyn in the 1960s to provide a reservoir for Liverpool, for example, was a significant political event, which changed the relationship between Wales and England and, some have argued, paved the way for devolution. But how much more important does that event seem when one sees photos of the people who lived in Capel Celyn—the pensioners, the children, their faces, their clothes—sitting on a bus on its way to Liverpool, to campaign to save their village. They raise their cups of tea and look through the camera lens at us from the years they're in, with all the reality of their experience etched into their faces. It is this connection, this empathy, which matters.

This is among the reasons why I adore the poems of Mair De-Gare Pitt. From its very first poem, its very first line, this collection focuses on the human and, through its brilliant lyricism, elevates the experiences it describes into something like beauty. The collection understands that the real way to political change is by moving people, by getting hold of their hearts, by writing memorably, and the poems do this again and again. Was there ever a more arresting opening line to a collection of poems than 'Today I am wearing a child's afternoon'?

This collection's three sections—'Children,' 'Women' and 'Society' —elegantly organise these poems' concerns. Blake, who knew a thing or two about making political points because of the reality of children's experience, presides over the poems of the first section as a sort of guardian presence. I was very taken by the moving focus in this section on difficulties of communication in poems such as 'A Child Tries to Read Aloud in Class' and 'Elective Mute.' These are highly empathetic pieces, and I was also struck by the irony of this experience being explored by a writer who communicates so beautifully—though difficulty and great success in communication are of course great companions. 'Black to Grey' is a poem which perfectly encapsulates how the South Wales Valleys have changed over a generation. Its last, ringing image speaks so eloquently for an experience which is being lived now on the streets of Newport and Newtown, Abersychan and Abertridwr.

The second section offers, arguably, even more powerful poems. 'The New Suit Man' takes a step towards the public poetry of writers like Auden and Betjeman, but at the heart of this section is a collection of unforgettable character portraits, documenting all sorts of female experiences. The poems range from the troubles of 'Our Lady of the Rags' and a 'Woman Sleeping Rough at Cardiff Castle'—a poem with an astonishing ending—to an old lady answering the phone, and astute and powerful depictions of motherhood in 'Respect' and 'Fruit-Picking at Berryhill Farm.'

In 'Society,' the collection opens out to explore a range of subjects. 'A Minister of Health' is a powerful poem of protest which reminded me of some of the political writing of Carol Ann Duffy, while 'Voices from the Great Flood' is a fabulously ambitious, multi-voiced poem. The collection concludes with a heartbreaking monologue about Grenfell which again shows this poet's understanding of the importance of putting people front and centre.

This collection is wonderfully illustrated by Jill Powell, the images and poems now endorsing each other, now opening each other up to new possibilities. It's a great thing to see a publisher putting together a sequence now of beautifully-written, wonderfully produced pamphlets, which seem to be doing something important and different in British poetry.

As for you, reader, mysterious or fedora'd ghost who may or may not be there, though I'm shouting this at you now, as if you're the magnolia or wallpapered wall of this room I'm writing in—I hope you'll love these poems as much as I do, and join with me in hoping that there will be many more of these poems for us to read, from a writer who is so refined, her voice so much her own, her poems so special, her concerns so significant. I'd say this collection is important because it's political. But I'll say more. It's important if you're human.

Contents

3. Society

1.
Children

Cheap as Chimney Sweeps

(After William Blake)

Today I am wearing a child's afternoon.
On my feet, flipping and flopping,
her glittering morning.

Her indigo hours, star-studded,
comfort my arms from chill.
I am dressed in her best.

Now her childhood lies soiled with my linen;
hangs limp on my washing line.

In the shadows cast on my summer lawn
I see her thin limbs twitch.

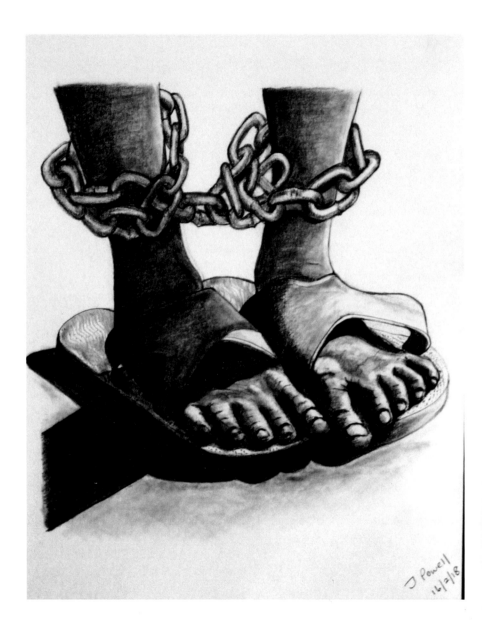

J Powell
16/2/18

A Child Tries to Read Aloud in Class

sca-ling
the words
like moun-tains
trudg-ing
through
syll-a-bles
he stum-bles
and falls;
their meaning, a kestrel in air,
hovers above his head,
watchful but unseen.

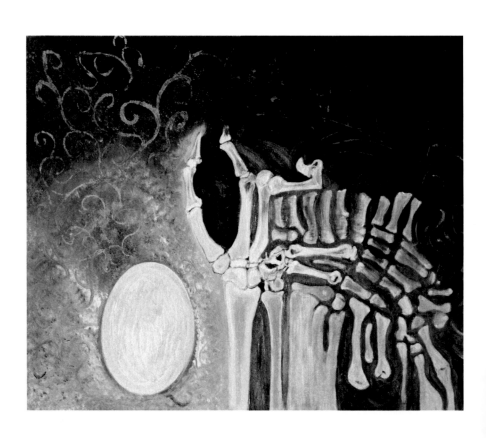

Asad's Circular Schema

In the Home Corner Cupboard
he is putting things in
he is taking things out
putting things in
taking things out.
While modelling his bowl
he pokes a stick
through the base
making a hole in the clay.
While moving to music
he is running around and around
and around and around.
While mark-making
he draws mandalas.
A chick hatched
from the egg of the Universe,
in the Home Corner Cupboard
he is putting things in
he is taking things out.

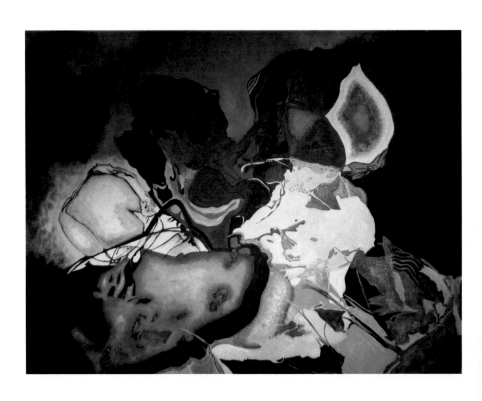

The Afon Llwyd is Flowing

a young mum feeds the ducks
throwing bread upon the moving waters

the river is storied with rippling
with hill-side rushing
swelling its whisperings

a young man, shattered when the steelworks shut
scuffs his boots along the dusty bank

its song floats key-changing
sunbursting ice-storming
majoring minoring

a schoolboy swings across white water
the rope frays and he's gone

its silver recalling
blank terror falling
into its swallowing

two bad boys sit silent for hours
sure they'll get a catch

it's laughing hiding
fleeting flitting
fish-life gliding

two good boys skid and hurl sticks.
"Look! That bird's like the sky!"

its banks are for sliding
for care-free kids splashing
for neon-blue kingfishers skimming

Black to Grey

Then
everything was grimed:
window sills, washing lines.
Everything was gritty:
teeth, eyeballs, fingertips.
Cable cars on the skyline
tipped slag on the hillside.
We slid on tin trays
and saw our toes when we bathed
clogged in dark dust.

Now
the litter that swirls
in the doorways
of boarded-up shops
is just grey.
And we have clean hands.

The Heavens' Rolling

The thin skim of ice on the pool
dissolves, and the child slips through.

In an instant his warm life cools.
He tumbles and somersaults slow
drifting down the black cold,
hair like a sun-burst unseen.
Ice-water squeezes his heart.

But in his veins, silvery crystals
halt the heavens' rolling
as stars blink with frost glint
and glitter like Christmas.

A Quiet Death

I'm playing underneath the table,
the cloth that hides me a fine tent.
Mam and Nanna are talking in whispers.
Their blurred words worry me.

I am eight. Someone has died.
I don't know who or how.
There will be a funeral that I won't attend.
No-one tells me what has happened.

I mutter stories to myself,
making shapes, making sense.
I stumble in my question-fall of sounds
as their silhouettes drift into silence.

Elective Mute

Words are sly, ink-black and full of holes
and some of them are pointed sharp as needles.
They stab me dumb as I fall through
the spaces in between.

My words mouth mimes
and hover, silent on thermals.
A cage of hot breath shuts them in.

My brain is taut with humming.
My tongue selects a silent power.

2.
Women

The New Suit Man

The new suit man's on the prowl.
He's on his way up.
He'll step on your head
in his new shoes.

You won't hear him
 creeping on the carpet
in his new shoes,
listening smartly in his new suit.

Don't sing so loud little birdie
or you'll be a feather in his cap.
He's the cat's whiskers
in his sleek new suit.

Our Lady of the Rags

A sickly-sweet cloud of cheap violet scent
masks her smell.

She shuffles past, flapping her mind
like a bird's broken wing.

Crowds freeze around her like water congealing
on a sea-bird's warm breast.

See where a young man sniggers
at her broken-backed shoes.

Winter evening curtains drawn at three.
Insistent minutes swirl in cups of tea.

Her mouth is stale with silence.
Her breath smells of loneliness.

Time in her fingers is tapping, tapping.
Time in her fingers is tapping

in ever present tense.

Cold Calling

An old woman sits; sips scalding tea,
struggles to stand. Her feet burn.
Pressing on chair backs, she staggers to the phone.

A pause. Machine-voice speaks.
She drops the receiver onto its cradle,
shuffles back to her seat.

An old woman sits; sips cooling tea.

The Lautrec Prints

Squint at them
muzzled in their bed-world
the ugliness of ageing in their tension.

Foreshortened
contorted
exhausted
corseted
and constrained
they jerk into work.

And we,
voyeurs of voyeurs
we peep
at the people
performing.

Patriarch

Lewis Price, gentleman, of Cwmcroythir in the parish of
Killycombe, 1740

Cross-patch geese stretch out their skinny necks
and swear at Dad in Welsh
as he drives them through
soft beds of warm pitch
then into sand
to sole their shiny new black boots.

Through the westerly drizzle they hike
their fourteen stony miles each day
from the Drovers' Arms
to the Red Cow
from the Red Cow
to the Black Ox
each dusk a pint and a pillow.

He sells the birds. Pays off the hands.
Rides home on the armchair back
of his bay Welsh cob
with a profit in his pocket.
The next batch wake the household
when they hear the clopping of his hooves.

When Dada dies,
to me, his daughter Gwen, he leaves
his second-best brass pan,

his chest of drawers and wooden vessels,
two pewter dishes from the dresser,
bedclothes (woollen blankets and a woven shawl)
and forty pounds
to furnish forth my life.

But my brother, also Lewis,
is disinherited
in favour of my other brother, John
who gets two hundred acres of land
with rights of common grazing,
brass, pewter and furniture.

Lewis gets ten pounds.

The Giant's Wife

"See them egg-shells, Jack?
Tip-toe across them, there's a love.
Hear him snore? He's in a black mist today.
Don't you wake him, now. He'll need to eat."

It's when you hear the bed-springs creak you have to stir.
My bulk's not quick to shift. If I could fly!
This churning dread's a weight.

"Now, see that bag of gold coins in his lap?
He'll never spend a penny piece."

He loves to rub his fingers through their buttery yellow.

"You need some cash, I know.
Sneak across, Jack, and grab it."

Then off you go, my boy, like a hare
skimming on snow.

"Don't fret over me. I'll plod on.
Big enough, ugly enough, me!
Go on, son, make yourself a life."

I'll pummel this pastry with strong arms.
A bit of steak and kidney'll do him good.

Crimson Lady

She is adorned with a necklace of tears
a smoky blouse of sighs,
with little tappy shoes that shine red
in the shadows.

Dainty blood-beads bracelet-dot her wrist
and hide in her scarlet skirt.

Sometimes she talks youth-speak
and paints its password on her mouth.
Tipsy lip-stick.

*

His key grinds
then wrenching, turns.
Her stomach churns.

The door swings;
china quivers.
She shivers.

The Fingers of My Curiosity

In her smooth, cool bucket bag are secrets.
They are nothing to do with me.
But the fingers of my curiosity
tip-toe across the table,
silently slip the buckle
and slide in.

There, in the darkness, is a letter.
The fingers of my curiosity pull it out;
but they cannot read.
They dive back in and scoop a lip-stick,
a bottle of Chanel, an empty purse.
Two sets of keys.

Why two?

The fingers of my curiosity
feel the Yale teeth, their prongs
so different from each other.

Blodeuwedd

She watches the squirrel, sharp-clawing bark,
the lizard lounging, lazy on stones,
the minnow wearing the water like silk.

Fritillaries bob in the turquoise
haze; the broom
is patched with purple.

In the sweet meadow, petals quiver,
shimmer in the warm breeze breath
and the mirage-making heat.

Dusk fills the field with shade.
Sky-lit hills scoop up the black.
All is becoming in the changing light.

Cool in its own shade
the oak beckons with long shadows.
Blodeuwedd dreams of day and wakes to dark.

A tussock couches, rabbit-like; rabbits crouch, still as tussocks
then sprint as air made animate
as living ghosts.

She conspires with the Moon
in silver fear.
Small creatures tremble and freeze.

Over sleeping flowers she glides
listening for rustling grasses,
scenting heartbeats in the darkness.

In the tarnished night she kills.
She swoops, wing-breath whispering
cold on the meadow-sweet.

She visits like a veil flitting through fingers.
She visits like a stream in flood.
She visits like a half-wish, like a scattered rose.

She is terrible in the darkness.
She is Kali, red tongue lolling.
She is Fury, twitching to snip.

As the long day rises
she is Eve, consuming night-knowledge.
At last, birth-star Mary, Mother of us.

Now she is Wendy.
She is fragrant Florence.
Beneath the cool starch, is she razors?

Dark falls again and she burns.
Now she is Wendigo, owl-beaked.
Why is she starving? Has she been fasting?

Dawn breaks on the hillside,
showers gleam like shot silk.
She raises her hand to her heavy hair.

Gardening Tips for Women

Not knowing is a tranquil bed
Suspecting is a spearing shoot
Denying is mulching it over
Doubting is the plant pricking through
Accepting is the gaudy flowering
and PAIN is the cutting of a blood-red bloom
and PAIN is shown in a cut-glass vase
and PAIN lasts while velvet petals drop; rot.

Dream of a garden green with possibilities
the seasons enclosed within trees
seed-catalogues painting the borders
a just-empty swing bumping the breeze
a secret arbour, a secret ardour.

A potting shed where mysteries of birth
chuckle in the darkness
a rock-pile where heathers
their thin fingers scrabbling
scale pebbles waving purple flags.

A garden-party of colour
 summers through the shrubbery
and wakes you with its chatter.

Beneath the pink azalea
a black and white cat's face
dappled with light and shade
follows a bobbing rabbit on the grass.

Respect

Hair like a raven's wing, eyes lined with night,
a freckled face pale as swans' down;
a husky voice and red-lipped laugh
attract the men. "Get lost, boys!"
Got my son. Everything's for him.
He's worth some aching limbs -
cleaning schools, waiting tables.
"Here's your lager, sir. Enjoy!"
No-one will laugh at him for crappy trainers.
I understand brand-names are just a con
(I did the course!) but I don't care.
I'll get in debt to buy him some respect.
He'll go to Disney; have a ManU bedroom.
My mother didn't have a clue, poor mouse.
I want to tear the world and feed him like a baby bird.

Woman Sleeping Rough at Cardiff Castle

Tomorrow, while I'm walking city streets
tourists will admire the tower's strength.
They leave. I swing back like a pendulum
clumsy with bags and blankets.
I throw my quilt among scuttling leaves
and wrap my smell around my shoulders.

Tomorrow I'll stand beneath a shower,
let the heat scour my skin.
Its sores and scabs will flake with suds
and streaks of grime that swirl around my toes.
Soaped and sweet I'll ride the roundabout
until my smile is sculpted into stone
back to the keep which keeps me safe.

I dream of scrabbling up its lichened walls
and scrubbing my hair with clouds.

Eve's Music

In the cacophony
        of her motherhood
from the gorgeous squeak
        of snow beneath tiny boots
to the blossomings of jazz
        from an upstairs window
her plump smile cherishes
        each treacherous moment
each sweetheart fall from grace.

What Men or Gods are These?

(After John Keats)

At Ancient Asine
high above the sea
lonely on a rock
watching the waves
in the pure warm silence of the sun

those tales of women ravished by gods
high above the sea
lonely on a rock
watching the waves
in the pure warm silence of the sun

are translated.
The woman is eternal.
The gods may be men.

Fruit-Picking at Berryhill Farm

Mothers and children come here.
The fruit stains our fingers like blood
with sharp sweetness.
Redcurrants, blackcurrants, raspberries, tayberries.

We wander through long grass,
hot sun on our necks.
Children grow fretful
but we are rapt,
enacting our childhood.

My mouth tastes of raspberries,
fruit soft as lips,
their redness silvered and dusted, gauzed in fine hairs,
their juice, when drupes burst on my tongue,
a sweet sharpness.

Sometimes a twitching worm.

3.
Society

A Minister of Health

His grammar deconstructs
when he is lying.
Sentence-structure disintegrates
when he is lying.
He stutters out evasions
ah-ah-ah
when he is misleading the public.
Lying to us, that is.
We could fall about laughing
but he holds the more-than-purse strings
on us when we are weak
                              ill
                                    mind-dark
                                          lost.

He can snip the strings
and watch us tumble.
He is IDIOT FATE
the blind SCISSORS-MAN
the *lying* AXE-MAN.
He stammers like a GENTLEMAN.
Sssnake-head.
"Angels and ministers of grace defend us."

A Caribbean Cruise

I *In the museum at Philipsburg, St Maarten*

This displaced skull
can now be repositioned.
The pointed teeth, you see,
point to his tribal origins.
This torso-less, brainless skull
so clearly out of place
is now re-homed in our thoughts.
We know where he belongs.
Yet he keeps his place in the history show
to show his displacement.

II *News from St Kitts*

Petroglyphs highlight in white paint
like a headline in the Sun
"Amerindian Massacre! Amerindian Massacre!"
Sub-heading on the signpost:
"Bloody Point"
and the text, its readability clear:
"Here the British soldiers killed the Indians."
Blood stains the river,
its threads pursuing
the fleeing kayaks
out of history.

III Nelson's Dockyard, Antigua

FOUR-SQUARE   LONDON   BRICK
WARMED   TO   MELLOW   GOLD
LIKE   SOLID GEORGIAN   PILES
SAILING   SHIPS   WEB-RIGGED
THEIR MASTS ACROSS THE LIGHT
BACKSHADOW AUCTIONBLOCKS
 BODIES   BOUGHT   AND SOLD
THE NETS TO CATCH THE LIGHT

Babylon the Great is Fallen

Apricots in a blue bowl.
Red rocks hunched like sunburnt shoulders.
The unbearable brightness of gold.
The bellowing of bulls.

After the fall, the busy-ness of life erupts;
there is rejoicing with cymbals;
limbs shuddering in dance.

A woman caresses the branch of a tree.
Its coolness is comfort.
Stones crumble to white dust in the sun.
Foliage scribbles a canopy against the heat.

Italian Retrospective

Like an old man, sky-full of memories,
Palazzo Blu invites us in
to wander through its layers of time.
TVs play flashes of mistakes on loops:
leather boots in flickering black and white,
the screen grainy with history like rheumy eyes.
Inlaid cabinets with secret drawers
hide whispers in dove-tailed spaces.

Regrets bow their heads in corners.
Galleries ring with grace-notes,
their triptychs in scarlet and gold-leaf
remembering love and loss and resurrection.

Like an old man, grateful for our time,
Palazzo Blu, head nodding, lets us go.

The Kingdom of Second Chances

In the Kingdom of Second Chances
clean slates are scribed with a new script;
cherries second-chewed with satisfaction.

In the Kingdom of Second Chances
the game is played on a level pitch
and the goal posts stand still as stone.

In the Kingdom of Second Chances
races are run straight as dies
and die is never said.

Voices from the Great Flood

*The Gwent Levels were flooded once in 1606. There are plans to
extend the M4 in this area.*

Once,
aurochs walked these grasslands; deer, wild pigs.
Then Roman soldiers drained the fens,
cultivated them to feed their garrisons.
Later, villages were built: a church,
and on its wall the watermark
of the first Great Flood.

Voice 1

Jackdaws clatter warnings.
A tall surge opaque with ruin
hurtles to my door
drowning our green sway.

I scramble up the stairs to fly its height.
It grabs my skirt, drags me down
into its splintered rage.

Voice 2

My maid child
sits calm among rushes,
her chubby fingers building with stalks.
Waters hurl through.
I scoop her up, my wide-eyed dear,

leap to the staircase; in my sudden strength
her four years' weight
light as a dandelion clock.
Before the waters claim her, speeding like a greyhound,
I tuck her safe upon a wooden beam.
Hold fast!
The flood sweeps me away.
She cries for cold.
A brown hen flutters up to keep her warm,
to give her comfort of a feathered breast
and keep her living.

Voice 3

Like Miriam
I cast my infant upon land
in a cradle floating upon flood,
steered by a tabby cat
that leaps from side to side
trying to keep the waters from her paws,
manoeuvring my babe round logs.
Her bassinet sticks safe,
caught in the mud where the bank is broke.

My husband and myself
perch on a branch
cawing for help like ragged crows.
We fly down into a tub,
our gowns flapping,
nothing but death before our eyes.

Now
grazing marsh, wetland and reen
sleep the wide sky's peace
dreaming the busy mystery
of otters, water-voles, stoats and foxes;
of meadow thistle, meadow rue, sedge and grasses.

A concrete wave would drown
in its nightmare ruin
all their green echoes.
All their green sway.

The Blues

She smashes through time-waves
riding her pleasure's lurch.
Droplets of ocean silver her path
as she carries the moon on her back.
Her calf drinks the riches
of her power,
The voices of her dead are singing
of the world's spinning,
singing of the Earth's breath.

The Breaking

I live in the next building.
Come on up.
I'm on the sixth floor.
From my balcony we could see them in silhouette
Just there. See?
We could hear them.
Still can.
We were sick scared and our hearts, our souls
Broke
As the tower, its black rags ripped like wings of crows
Broke
And their lives, brimful of dreams and hopes
Broke
It was a vision of hell, somebody said,
The flames flickering like Satan's tongue,
Like his forked tail.
But I think the devils are still here,
Still with us.
Still in one piece.

Ripples

Breeze on a still pool.
God, like dark matter, unseen,
passes through like breath.

Notes by the author and artist

The general theme pursued throughout this collection is the impact of personal and political power on people's lives.

Children are subject to the abuse of power in commerce, in education and in the physical world, because of their vulnerability. However, they also possess a power of their own, whether through their very innocence, or through refusing to play the games they are sometimes pressurised to take part in. They insist on expressing their own creativity. Women, too, have suffered in the workplace, in the home, in relationships and in the ownership of property, through the exploitation of their perceived weakness. But like children they have developed their voice, and discovered individual and collective strengths, sometimes in surprising ways.

Power Play also explores our vulnerability as a society, to the rationing of resources, to enslavement, to the effects of war, to criminality, and the call to use what power we have—including the spiritual powers we can call on—to liberate others as well as ourselves, and protect the natural world around us all.

Mair De-Gare Pitt

I first met Mair when I joined her Creative Writing Class. At that time she was enquiring if anyone knew of a local artist who might be interested in illustrating a pamphlet of her poetry. Mair's female-biased power poems resonated with my surreal approach to art and we gelled. Consequently I agreed to collaborate with her on this project. The rest is history or to be more specific an illustrated pamphlet.

I really enjoyed the challenge of bringing Mair's poetry into the visual spectrum, the merging of two art forms and maximising the impact of the themes expressed. A wide range of art techniques were used e.g. pencil, oil, acrylic, watercolour, collage and photography, with each poem being paired to a sympathetic medium.

Jill Powell

Cheap as Chimney Sweeps was prompted by the poems of William Blake who wrote about child exploitation in late 18th century London in his series of poems concerning the small boys who were forced to work as chimney sweeps. It seemed to me that child labour was an issue that still prevails. *M.D-G.P.*

The accompanying image, **Shackled Childhood**, was created specifically for the poem showing a child's feet in adult flip flops, with their ankles in chains. *J.P.*

Asad's Circular Schema refers to the stage in the development of the young child where movement is dominated by circular or oval shapes. The mandala and egg imagery refers to Hindu theories of the creation of the universe and to Christian imagery of new life (as in Easter/oestrus). Asad himself was a little Muslim boy—so the poem unites three belief systems. *M.D-G.P.*

The accompanying image, **Osteo Egg**, is an abstract of a multi-fingered hand giving birth to an egg, a promise of a new start. *J.P.*

The Afon Llywd is Flowing. The Afon Llwyd (Grey River) runs through the county of Torfaen. When industry was dominant it was known as the dirtiest river in Wales. It is now clear, but has left behind unemployment. It retains its own power over life and death. *M.D-G.P.*

The accompanying image, **Alone in the Universe**, was originally produced for an exhibition in The Worker's Gallery in response to a poem by Mike Church. *J.P.*

The Heavens' Rolling was prompted by a newspaper article about a young boy who fell through ice and was thought to have died. The low temperature slowed his metabolism to such an extent, however, that he survived. The poem hints at the correlation between science and religion. *M.D-G.P.*

The accompanying image, **Phoenix Boy**, was created for the poem showing a young boy arising from the lake with ice crystal wings. *J.P.*

Patriarch is based on the will of my ancestor, Lewis Price. The will summarily disinherits the elder son in favour of the younger with no explanation. The daughter is not bequeathed land or property. *M.D-G.P.*

The accompanying image, **One Eyed God**, was an attempt to paint the face of God. But, the painting turned into a question of faith, and religion. It asks us to question the integrity of the Patriarch. *J.P.*

Blodeuwedd. The Welsh myth of Blodeuwedd is used to explore the male construct of the perfect woman, and the reality which finally wins through. In the story, Blodeuwedd is created by the wizard Gwydion out of flowers: oak, broom and meadowsweet. Once the beautiful woman is called into existence, however, she discovers another side to her nature, which is not so compliant. Eventually Gwydion gives her the shape of an owl. *M.D-G.P.*

A Caribbean Cruise makes reference to slavery, and visits the islands of St Maarten, St Kitts and Antigua. *M.D-G.P.*

The accompanying image, **Tardis Traveller**, was originally created as part of my degree show and shows a modern take on Memento Mori-themed paintings. *J.P.*

Italian Retrospective. Through the image of an old man, the poem looks at the recent history of Italy and its adoption of fascism for a time. It explores regret but also acknowledges beauty reated in the past. *M.D-G.P.*

The accompanying image, *After Chirico*, was originally created as an attempt to copy the style of artist Giorgio De Chirico. *J.P.*

Babylon the Great is Fallen looks at how, when a civilization is destroyed, both the positive and negative things associated with it are lost. Finally, those who are most vulnerable suffer. *M.D-G.P.*

The accompanying image, *Hanging Basket*, was originally created as an abstract in green and gold. *J.P.*

Voices from the Great Flood. The stories used here come from texts which document experience of the flood of 1605/6 which affected the Gwent Levels. It draws a parallel between the power of nature, which is uncontrollable, and the power of governments to make decisions which may be detrimental. *M.D-G.P.*

Ripples. This again draws a link between science and religion. It was prompted by an article in National Geographic which explored the possibility of invisible dark matter flowing through concrete matter. *M.D-G.P.*

The accompanying image, *Moon Dancing*, shows a whale and her calf dancing in the moonlight under a hunter's moon. *J.P.*

Voyeur was created for the poem, **The Lautrec Prints**, and shows a copy of a Lautrec print viewed through a keyhole.

Secrets and Lies, which accompanies the poem **The Fingers of My Curiosity,** was created for the poem and lets us imagine what could be behind the padlocked door.

Prisoner of Silence was created for the poem **A Quiet Death**, and shows a soldier suffering from PTSD obviously in distress. In the folds of his trousers can be seen the outline of two women.

A String of Beads was created for the poem **Crimson Lady**. The woman in the painting is the blood in the fragile cup and the beads are made of blood.

Crimson Petals was created for the poem, **Gardening Tips For Women**.

Best of the Best was created for the poem **Respect**. A baby bird is in a nest of logos from wealthy advertisers crying out for real sustenance.

Rough Rugby was created for the poem **Woman Sleeping Rough At Cardiff Castle.**

All That Jazz was created for the poem **Eve's Music** and shows a woman caught up in the power of the music.

Emancipation was created for the poem **What Men Or Gods Are These?**. The idea was taken from the sculpture *Abduction of The Sabine Women* by Giambologna, 1581-83, in marble. The top of the statue I have captured in paint and shows the marble head and arm of the woman becoming flesh and her hair in a modern style which alludes to the 21st century woman throwing off the shackles of male oppression.

Into Infinity, which accompanies the poem **The Kingdom of Second Chances**, was created after my degree to show how the stress of the year was dissipating.

Into The Blue, which accompanies the poem **Voices from the Great Flood**, was created as part of my National Diploma in response to W.H. Auden's poem, 'Stop all the Clocks'. It is a textile work using parts of clocks and white wool and cotton.

Hand of God, which accompanies the poem **The Blues** was created in response to the belief of many Christians that God's return to this world is imminent.

Goya's Grenfell Hell was created for the poem **The Breaking**. I have incorporated the burned-out tower into the body of a devil. This idea originated from *Saturn Devouring His Son* by Goya.

J.P.

Mair De-Gare Pitt has taught English and Creative Writing for many years and has published poetry widely in magazines and anthologies. She has been successful in competitions for poetry, short stories and playwriting, and had published studies on Indian poet, Rabindranath Tagore, and children's writer, Alfred Bestall. She runs a local drama group in Cwmbran, and is a member of Red Poets, taking part in readings in South Wales, where she lives and works. She is thrilled to work with artist, Jill Powell. She is married, with children and grandchildren who give her hope for the future.

Jill Powell is a mixed media artist based in Cwmbran, South Wales. As a mature student, with a work background in Medical Laboratory Sciences, she explored her lifelong love of Art and graduated from the University of South Wales with a BA in Art Practice (Hons). Since then she has exhibited at The Workers Gallery in Ynyshir, RCT and Pontypool Museum, Gwent. Her art is often surreal in nature, having evolved from her feelings and dreams. She often utilises a mixed media approach and my art practice up until now has incorporated humour, surrealism, sculpture, animation and the exploration of alternative realities.

Jonathan Edwards' first collection, *My Family and Other Superheroes* (Seren, 2014) received the Costa Poetry Award and the Wales Book of the Year People's Choice Award. It was shortlisted for the Fenton Aldeburgh First Collection Prize. He lives in Crosskeys, South Wales, and works as a teacher.

CULTURE MATTERS

Publications

Recent publications from Culture Matters, available from http://www.culturematters.org.uk/index.php/shop-support/ our-publications

arise! by Paul Summers

This pamphlet-length poem celebrates the rich heritage and culture of mining communities, which is expressed so vibrantly and colourfully in the marches, the banners, the music and the speeches at the Durham Miners' Gala. It invokes the collective and co-operative spirit of past generations of men and women who worked and struggled so hard to survive, to build their union, and to organise politically to fight for a better world.

Arise! also celebrates the new, resurgent spirit in the Labour Party, led by Jeremy Corbyn, and the renewal of support for socialist solutions to the country's growing economic and social problems.

It's wonderful to see the proud history of the Durham Miners' Gala represented in this powerful poem. Paul Summers has managed to capture the spirit of the Miners' Gala and its central place in our movement's mission to achieve 'victory for the many, and not the few'.
—**Jeremy Corbyn**, leader of the Labour Party

10% of the proceeds of sales of this book will go to the Durham Miners' Association Redhills Appeal, to help turn Redhills into a cultural hub for the area.

Poetry on the Picket Line
an anthology edited by Grim Chip and Mike Quille

Poetry with principles. Poetry with a point. Poetry on the picket line. That's where it should be.

—Billy Bragg

This anthology of poems is sponsored by PCS, RMT and the TUC (London, East and South EastE)Poetry on the Picket Line sounds a bit unlikely, but it works. It's a squad of writers prepared to turn up on picket lines and read poetry. Something a bit different, and it usually goes down well.

The poets do what it says on the tin. They turn up at pickets and demos and read poems—with a mic, without a mic, through a bullhorn, whatever. Pickets are generally pretty pleased and surprised to see them. They appreciate the support, and some of them even appreciate the poetry!

It matters because it brings poetry onto picket lines and picket lines into poetry. Real people connecting with real poetry in the real world. That's got to be a good thing!

This anthology of poems from PotPL is sponsored by trade unions: PCS, RMT and TUC (London, East and South East). All proceeds from the sale of this book will go into strike funds.

The Combination by Peter Raynard

Peter Raynard has written a remarkable new long poem to mark the 200th anniversary of Marx's birth, and the 170th anniversary of the publication of the Communist Manifesto.

Like the Manifesto, it protests the injustice and exploitation which is integral to capitalism, and the growing gap between capitalism's productive potential and the unequal distribution of its benefits. And like that Manifesto, it is a dynamic and powerful piece of writing—pungent, oppositional and unsettling.

This poetic coupling is something else. It's a re-appropriation, a reclamation, a making sing. It's bolshie (yes, in every sense), provocative and poignant too. It takes the Manifesto back from all that is dead, dry and terminally obfuscated. It's a reminder of reality, the flesh on the theory. It gives Marx to those of us who need him most. Not just relevant, but urgent. Not just angry, but hopeful.

—**Fran Lock**

Muses and Bruises by Fran Lock and Steev Burgess

Fran Lock's socialist poetry weaves psychological insight and social awareness into themes of poverty, mental health problems, sexual abuse, domestic violence and political struggle. It is vivid, lavish and punchy, combining a deep sense of anger and injustice with vulnerable empathy and compassion.

The fragmented yet coherent collages of Steev Burgess complement and enhance those meanings perfectly. His images dance with the poems, singing together about muses and bruises, fantasy and reality—grind and grime with a lick of glitter.

The Things Our Hands Once Stood For by Martin Hayes

Martin Hayes is the only British poet who writes consistently and seriously about work, and about the insanity of a society where employees are seen merely as mere 'hands' to be employed and to make money for their employer.

Work is what most of us have to do, and the workplace is where most of us spend a large part of our lives. Work should be about creatively transforming the world around us to meet all our needs, but it isn't. For the many, work is hard, precarious, poorly paid, unsatisfying and alienating, and constantly threatened by automation. Workers 'never get to share in its profits/but always seem to get to share/in its losses'. Why? Because of the few who own their labour 'squeezing away at people's lives like they were plastic cups'.

The clear message of his poetry is that those who do the work should own, control, and benefit fully from it. They should, in the last words of the last poem, 'start the revolution that will change everything', and show that 'all of our fingertips combined/ might just be the fingertips/that keep us and this Universe/ stitched together'.

A Third Colour by Alan Dunnett and Alix Emery

Through the sheen of vivid, simple narratives and vignettes, we glimpse more disturbing, ambivalent themes of alienation, dislocation and suffering, the psychological fallout of anxiety in modern capitalist culture.

A Third Colour is a book of visionary, poetic parables and dystopian, uneasy images. It is a principled and skilful expression of, and protest against, the world we live in.

On Fighting On! The Bread and Roses Poetry Anthology 2017

An anthology of poems from the Bread and Roses Poetry Award 2017, sponsored by Unite.

We sponsored the first Bread and Roses Poetry Award because we believe that our members, and working people generally, have an equal right to join in and enjoy all the arts, and other cultural activities. We believe we should be able to afford them, get to them, and enjoy them, and that art should seek to engage with all sections of the community. Working-class people face a continual cultural struggle to defend our cultural commons, to keep cultural activities open to the many, not the few.

—**Len McCluskey**, General Secretary of Unite

Bring the Rising Home! by Mike Jenkins and Gustavius Payne

Weaving through both poems and images are themes of individual isolation and alienation, and the urgent need to recognize that collective action is necessary to change the conditions of working people. Mike Jenkins's vivid, lyrical poems work together with Gustavius Payne's bold, striking, and deeply sympathetic paintings, complementing each other perfectly.

Here is a poetic and painterly union of two socialist Welsh artists who, in their own brilliant, artistic way, are interpreting and changing the world—bringing the Rising home!

The Earth and the Stars in the Palm of Our Hand
by Fred Voss

I want to change the world, I want to strike the spark or kick the pebble that will start the fire or the avalanche that will change the world a little.

— **Fred Voss**

Fred Voss has been a metalworker in workshops in Long Beach, California for over 30 years. His poems are set in the world of work —the workers and bosses in the machine shop where he works, the social usefulness of the products they make, the alienation aggression and camaraderie of the workplace and the relationship of work to the wider world. The poems sympathetically criticise that world, but also envision a better, fairer world, in and out of the workplace.

Everyone can see the growing inequality, the precarious and low paid nature of employment, the housing crisis in our cities, the divisions and inequalities between social classes, the problems of obesity, drink and drugs, and the sheer everyday struggle to pay the bills for many working people.

In this situation, Fred Voss is like a prophet. He is warning us of the consequences of the way we live, he is telling truth to power, and he is inspiring us with a positive vision of a possible—and desirable—socialist future.

—**Len McCluskey**, General Secretary of Unite

Lugalbanda—Lover of the Seed by Doug Nicholls

Produced as a fundraiser for the Free Ocalan campaign, this new version of a 5,000 year old poem speaks out afresh to our times, with lyrical skill and political relevance.

Lugalbanda, a heroic figure from the Sumerian era, the first civilisation to invent writing, the wheel, law, architecture and irrigation, personifies the amazing creative force at the heart of human culture.

At a time when neoliberal capitalism and its associated ideologies seek to deny and destroy the sense of human agency and labour as the source of all social change, and of all our cultural and material wealth, Lugalbanda reminds us of our deepest, most distinctive social and creative natures, our stupendous power to create and destroy, and the joys of communication and social interaction.

On Fighting On! The Bread and Roses Poetry Anthology 2017

An anthology of poems from the Bread and Roses Poetry Award 2017, sponsored by Unite.

We sponsored the first Bread and Roses Poetry Award because we believe that our members, and working people generally, have an equal right to join in and enjoy all the arts, and other cultural activities. We believe we should be able to afford them, get to them, and enjoy them, and that art should seek to engage with all sections of the community. Working-class people face a continual cultural struggle to defend our cultural commons, to keep cultural activities open to the many, not the few.

—**Len McCluskey**, General Secretary of Unite

Slave Songs and Symphonies
by David Betteridge and Bob Starrett

Slave Songs and Symphonies is an ambitious, beautifully crafted collection of poems, images and epigraphs. It's about human history, progressive art and music, campaigns for political freedom, social justice and peace. Above all it's about the class and cultural struggle of workers 'by hand and by brain' to regain control and ownership of the fruits of their labour.

David Betteridge's poems are leftist, lyrical, and learned, infused with sadness and compassion for the sufferings of our class, the working class. They are also inspired by visionary hope, and a strong belief that our class-divided society and culture can be transformed by radical politics and good art—and by radical art and good politics.

Bob Starrett's drawings are much more than illustrations. They dance with the poems, commenting on them as well as illustrating them. They are like Goya's drawings in their dark, ink-black truthfulness and their intimate knowledge of suffering and Blake's 'mental fight'. Like the poems, they express and resolve the struggles they depict.

Slave Songs and Symphonies tells the story of how slave songs become symphonies—and helps makes it happen. It is not just about class and cultural struggle—it is class and cultural struggle.